Crits

"These are really beautiful p[...]
to shedding a tear on reading [...]
Osborn, Kent

"We have dipped into the sonnets - they are beautiful! We will continue reading during our next visit." **Helen Hall, Exeter**

"Many thanks for sending me a copy of your sonnets dedicated to Margaret - beautiful and sad at the same time." **Christine Miles, Kent**

Poems Writ for Lublu:

A Tragedie in Fifty-one Sonnets

David Gordon Rose

RoseTintedSpecs Imprint

Copyright Matters

Poems Writ for Lublu: A Tragedie in Fifty-one Sonnets are
51 sonnets taken from the author's body of poetry. Twenty-five
of the 51 were first published in 2003.

Cover image "Lublu's Song" and all interior images courtesy of
Rose Photo Archive except for the images on pages 11 and 20
by kind permission of Ludmila Stiebner. The rag dolls Lublu
and Pierrot were created by the late Sigrid Spenser.

ISBN 978-0-9544518-1-3 (paperback)
ISBN 978-0-9927057-4-9 (.mobi/ Kindle)

RoseTintedSpecs Imprint
Publisher: David G. Rose
Butchers Farm, Molash, Kent, United Kingdom
www.rosetintedspecs.com
email: publisher@rosetintedspecs.com

Printed in the US and UK. British-English spelling is used in
this book. Font licensing correct at time of publication

Contents

Introduction

This book of fifty-one sonnets follows a love story over three-and-a-half years. I met Margaret (Lublu, or the Lady in the book) in passing in the early 1990s, a woman with the beauty of a young Elizabeth Taylor and unforgettable green eyes. This may sound clichéd but her picture in my Dedication at the end of the book will give you the idea.

With typical modesty she said this likeness had been a problem all her life, from her schoolfriends telling her the actress in the film (National Velvet) showing in the village looked just like her, to a complete stranger embracing her spontaneously in a Limoges street saying she was the most beautiful woman she had ever seen.

I met the Lady again in Autumn 1999 when some Austrian clients asked if I could take them to the house, King's Court, where they were dining that evening. I recognised her immediately. She was embarrassed she didn't remember me but invited me in with the group for dinner in a typical gesture of hospitality. We met again by chance the following weekend at the house of a mutual friend. This happened once more near Christmas.

Recently divorced and living in digs I baked the Lady a birthday/ Christmas cake. I was invited to her New Year gathering but this was cancelled because she and I and many others were struck down with the serious Australian Flu of that winter.

The Lady was still frail on Valentine's Day but she said the notes on health tips and thanks or wishing well I left in her post box were a great help. I knew many of her friends by then from weekend dinners and from being part of the "First Tuesday" group, the day every month when those of us single or widowed got together at her house bringing wine and a contribution to the meal.

I first truly missed the Lady when away in Stockholm in April and penned a second sonnet, one more thoughtful than that thanking her for an Easter dinner and a local Spanish flamenco evening. The effect was dramatic on a woman who read Shakespeare incessantly. It was not the plays she was dipping into.

With little experience of writing poetry I was, nevertheless, well aware of how hard it is to express yourself in verse and was taken aback at the level of artistry in Shakespeare's sonnets. I don't know how other authors react when hearing or reading them for the first time. I wept. This would be the medium in which I would express my thoughts to this lady beyond the more ordinary, shall I say, declaration of love by letter.

In a suitably grand gesture after the delight with which my first efforts were received I pledged to write one more than Shakespeare did to his love(s).

The intimidation of her well-read Complete Works remained but I got to grips with themes, variation in metre and the occasional parody. As an author the agonising over my offerings word by word and line by line remains my best writing discipline.

They were a joy, she said generously about the early sonnets and she looked forward to receiving more. Later, she would look at me in silence after reading a new poem, the pleasure ibeing obvious. I made a slip case for the cards in which I inserted the poems., some of which are shown in the book. The Complete Works was discreetly put away.

I wrote fifty-one of my goal of one hundred and fifty-five sonnets. The Lady died in the Spring of 2003.

* * *

Poems Writ for Lublu
A Tragedie in Fifty-one Sonnets

Sonnet I
Joy Lane, 24 April 2000

'Tis plain clear there's no such word as never
when I dost vow to dote on thee for ever.
But though I muse the Master's imitation,
certain do I know my limitation!
I thank thee for a fulsome, homely fête,
Playful Maiden well and truly met,
to whom is penned this humble rhyming part
from one full gone to win his Lady's heart.
To dine the morrow I now long with hunger,
most to feast my eyes on you, my Dreamer.
Tortillas wait, I say! We are come soon
to dip into a lusty Spanish spoon.
'Tis obvious late, this sonnet's bound to slip!
I bid thee well tonight from heart and lip.

Sonnet 1. was my thanks for Easter weekend at the Lady's house and an invitation to a flamenco evening at a local restaurant. This was my first sonnet and far more satisfying to compose than the notes I had dropped into her post box since the Autumn. We were still smiling and having dinner together regularly at her house, King's

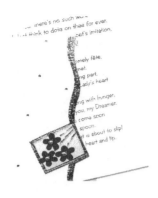

Court and alternating cooking it.

"Yes, yes!" she exclaimed, in wonder, I like to think, on reading the poem.

"Er, no," I countered. It failed as a sonnet and prompted me to look more carefully at its structure over the next few days.

Sonnet II
Stockholm, 30 April

So hard, the tender touch of our embrace,
to feel each other's gently beating hearts
then prised away, you always full of grace
while I did want to reach those deeper parts.
So cruel then, your whispered promised tryst,
your fleeting fingers sealing lips untold
except I must come back and you insist
we will be one and I, you will behold.
So chilling now, your eyes of molten green
warming Arctic waters dark and deep
that twilit April eve where swans do preen
and salmon pink 'cross royal blue do leap.
Now within your private gaze, to bare
my soul to you in trust I am to dare.

10

Sonnet 2. *Margaret accompanied me shopping before my trip to Sweden. It was the first time we had done anything together out of the house on our own except for walking the dogs along the sea front. I was staying at weekends in the guest room at King's Court partly to help the Lady with her almost weekly dinners for friends. As I left the house on Saturday morning she handed me a card for reading on the flight.*

"You might look at tall, blonde Scandinavian beauties but please don't bring one home!" she wrote.

I was taken by surprise. She was one step ahead of me. This card and my cards and Sonnets 1. and 2. were the turning point in our relationship.

Sonnet III
Argyle Road, 3 May

Now my Love resides within my head
softly humming tunes and chasing themes.
'Tis joyful that this Lady is well-read
like the finest wines and sweetest dreams
such, nightly in my mind I'm wooed and dined,
her presence clear the spur of hand and heart.
With laughter, love and music intertwined,
smiles, these words and she are now my art.
Tonight abroad, though home's in warmer ports,
'tis Delight that guards my whetted palette.
Her Mistress will return to fire my thoughts
and once again I'll sip a mellowed claret.
Who needs Gallic charm with ripest cheese?
Just come home to us, my Love, please.

Sonnets 3. and 4. While I was in Sweden the Lady was in Paris with her friend Sara. I didn't know she was to be introduced to a recently widowed doctor. I house-sat King's Court on my return. My dinner for the Lady, with a sauce I created for her was badly timed because she had a huge parting lunch in Paris.

She was touched at my efforts

*looking after the dogs, composing
a sonnet and a song "Springtime
is for You and Me" set in the
Paris she loved. The 'blind date'
she remarked, was a non-event.*

*I finished Sonnet 4. the day after
her return while waiting in the
theatre foyer for a Music Society
concert to end. I wanted to walk
her back across town at dusk.*

Sonnet IV
King's Court, 4 May

Flitting siskin, finch and thrush yet grown
'cross mellowed brick touched ochre, dun and green,
I looked, my Love, as they but you had flown.
'Twas I, *tout seul,* who felt their warming sheen.
As these gentle friends did grace this garden,
I in contemplation watched them free
and played a little tune and begged their pardon
though this moody food sustained us three.
We did wait, us lads and pine somewhat,
Bertie Boy, d'Arcy Dog and I.
This tranquil corner was our restless lot
while patiently we waited you to spy.
Missing not is bird or bee or dove,
it is you. Welcome home, my Love.

13

Sonnet 5. *also relates to the 'competition.' I was trying very hard and lamented, perversely I suppose, being unable to express myself as well as Shakespeare.*

"It will take time," the Lady said kindly, insisting my efforts so far were well worth it.

She had a strong faith. I don't but making reference to it in poetry is perfectly acceptable, surely?

Sonnet V
Joy Lane, 9 May

A bee or not? Perhaps two bees?
No need to question nature's spoil
when sun and scented May are one at ease,
for you, my honeyed dream, the perfect foil.
Three ewes or four? Just you I need, not sheep.
Alone at night I count those wispy smiles
and only when they've kissed my eyes I sleep
content your tenderness my body fills.
Such joy abounds in slumber's dance and play
from softest lips and lambs and humming bees.
But those days abroad you were away,
the nights, the stars, became the nursery frieze
and I did wish, as you did pray at Chartres,
for the blessing of our Lord and Master.

Sonnet VI
Joy Lane, 13 May

No perfumed hedge or heady sun-warmed spray
or dew-dropped May and lilac-blossomed morn
prepared me for my Lady's scented way
down sweet damp paths that soft-sung golden dawn.
No shimmered cloth or finest damask thread
as caravanned an endless starlit age
did compare those melting eyes I read
as love is scribed on history's precious page.
And as we stepped those paths that perfect morn,
just as the softest smells and sweetest milk
do stir the senses of the newly-born,
I felt in her the timeless touch of silk.
Let not go my hand, my gentle Love,
lest I do miss a moment in this grove.

Sonnet 7. commemorates the Lady's husband's death. It was one of his tales. She had sobbed a few days earlier at his anniversary dinner. I came around the table to comfort her and she grasped my hand, to the surprise of some.

I suggested a day-trip to France during the week. We had a late lunch, danced in the aisles of Carrefour and bought wine. The Lady said she looked forward to returning to France with me.

Sonnet VII
Joy Lane, 22 May

A fellow forced his pig and it expired.
There's a moral here; the pig has gone
as death does want but where a man's admired,
with conscience clear this deed he'll ne'er have done.
All us living things pass soon enough
and if, transcendent, charity's unknown
this can beget a death unduly tough,
sad, oft tragic, empty and alone.
I am learning things from one so dear,
from one loved truly now just as before.
This theme is thus to both you here
whose love lies either side Death's closèd door,
whose love remains a credit to all men;
this verse to you, Margaret and Ken.

Sonnet VIII
Joy Lane, 27 May

Lublu's pale and barely smiles today.
Twinkle-eyed with dancing shoes and flute
Pierrot calls but knows she's far away,
fragile-lipped in party frock and mute,
her fine black hair across the pillow spread.
In a moment of *douleur* he's lost
with garden friends concerned that she's abed
as though the courtyard's once again in frost.
He guards her as a soldier, lest befall
the nursery bogeys pull her arm again,
with lacy gloves and finest linen shawl,
Mistress of the yard, the band, the pen.
Sweet mien returned, his hand to hold
but will tomorrow she blow hot or cold?

Sonnet 8. *is the first referring the Lady's childhood toys with the rag dolls Lublu, her musician suitor Pierrot and other King's Court characters. The dolls pictured in this book were created by artist Sigrid Spenser, my landlady at Joy Lane, commissioned for the Lady's birthday later that year. She grabbed Pierrot from the box and*

clutched him to her chest, whereas I wanted to hold Lublu. Sigrid knew the Lady and had made an uncanny likeness.

These characters and the nursery scenario added a dimension in which I could express my thoughts in a lighter way. The Lady was enchanted and I penned another sonnet a few days later developing the theme further.

I had recently told her, gently, she was occasionally moody and regretted it immediately. She said she sometimes deserved reproval but didn't tell me she had low blood pressure problems and anaemia. Despite having no energy she troubled to take the car out and buy a new dressing gown for me for my Wednesday visit. She was also admitted to hospital for two days for a check-up.

Sonnet IX
King's Court, 1 June

June's a-bursting in the wings today,
courtyard friends did wave the music wand
and birds join in the early morning fray
to watch in wonder Pierrot and the band.
There's a double reason for the show
with Lublu home again all dressed anew.
Golly's going to sing and take the bow
and all the toys will join in May's *adieu*.
The fairy band played on a heady pace
applauded long by gentle King's Court Elves.
These Toytime sounds evoke the magic place
where friendly, cuddly toys can be themselves.
Lublu welcomes Season's daughter, June.
About her arm she's truly o'er the moon.

Sonnet 9. *The Lady felt better after treatment and a rest from a social life that was taking its toll. I began to take over much of the chores of shopping and preparing dinner for groups of friends. I was still lodging on the other side of town but was now the Lady's companion midweek and at weekends.*

Sonnet X
Joy Lane, 8 June

Since Moon and Mother Earth embraced of old
the Rosy Orb has fiery passion thrust
and spread its glowing hand of fingers gold
'cross endless empty morns of cosmic dust.
Then has it also slipped the gift of night,
such, impassioned lovers calm and gaze
'twixt pleasure sighs and whispers tight
a myriad of silent stars ablaze,
to dream celestial paths paralleled
through stars flung far across Elysium's field,
a firmament so eagerly beheld,
a Milky Way laid fresh as loved ones yield.
Through Heaven's age-old paramour's delight
we will go far our star-gazed lovers' flight.

Sonnet XI
Mt. Ephraim, 22 July

Tonight my Love's alone in pleasant sleep
with softest rain and oft-remembered faces,
tracing hedge and vale and sturdy sheep
recalling joyful, former happy places.
In her father's land, his loving daughter
rests again with precious childhood thoughts,
roaming greenest hills in youthful laughter,
treading flaxen sand on savoured walks.
Courted here through honeysuckled days
by noble horse and lamb and Summers long
she grew and learnt of love's endearing ways
in a rugged, passioned land of song.
Though she rests that distant windswept fold
she will return for me to love and hold.

Sonnet 11. The Lady went to visit her aunt for a few days in Pembrokeshire. I had answered the 'phone a few days earlier and Auntie was a little confused thinking I was Ken, though it had been eleven years since his death.

After Margaret's return we were sitting in the grounds of Mount Ephraim in Kent enjoying the outdoor concert while I finished this welcome home sonnet.

Sonnet XII
Joy Lane, 22 August

Today my Love returned befriended places,
beacon beaming sea and snowy mount,
smile-emblazoned, lighting waiting faces,
living store of love one cannot count.
Begone all cares and woes and tired malaise!
Warmed a-brimming now a treasure chest
I'm just dazzled by her jewel-like gaze
and love that shines from one so beauty-blest.
Time did slow the ticking metronome,
clockwork stars did stop and prick the hours,
'twas such a joy that she did hurry home,
Bayrisch fresh with Passion Play and flowers,
launching on the way her thousand ships
but mine to dwell upon those sweetest lips.

Notes Sonnet 12. The Lady returns with Sara from a trip to Austria to see the Oberammergau Passion Play staged only every ten years. She was bubbling with enthusiasm about the production and the Austrians I had met on my first evening at King's Court the previous Autumn.

She had wished I was there to enjoy the spectacle with her.

Notes Sonnet 13. *I received birthday cards from two of the Lady's closest friends. It had taken a while to be accepted as her love. Almost a year since we met we were still not living together. An acceptable courtship, I would say.*

Sonnet XIII
Joy Lane, 16 September

It's Pierrot's birthday treat today
arranged with special Lublu love and care
but Pierrot saw her slip away
and miss the jollity and wholesome fare.
She returned with gifts and friends as planned
and eager country folk now joined the fun.
They all loved the King's Court fairy band
and crowed and mooed and pranced in glorious sun.
Then Teddy brought a lovely cake to share
and Lublu smiled and soft embraced her *Beau.*
Golly raised the baton for the pair
and all did hearty sing until dusk's show.
Pierrot held his Lublu's hand back home,
pleased she whispered him to be her own.

Sonnet XIV
King's Court, 24 September

I caress my Love from slumber sweet,
stirring her this dampened English morn.
We are soon away, the sun to greet,
transported there before tomorrow's dawn.
Hand-in-hand and making our escape
with pensive smile at sky like watery broth,
to venture crinkled noon and gorgeous grape
and evenings cooing 'cross a lanterned cloth;
from limestone bake and herbs cicadas play,
through whisper sleep and shuttered village cool,
la promesse, pâtisserie, café
et dejeuners gallique to make us drool.
Ma raison d'être, Amour, mon Billet-doux,
is to share this *ambience* with you.

Sonnets 14. and 15. *This was my first attempt at introducing another language into a poem. I haven't seen much of this. Maybe there is a good reason.*

For our first trip away we booked a week in the Dordogne travelling by coach. We hired a car locally. The Lady was, as ever, a delightful companion.

In Paris I discovered she had many friends and that she had long considered buying a small apartment. She mooted months later she pay the deposit and I pay the mortgage. The idea was another step forward in our relationship. It was not to come to fruition.

Sonnet XV
Paris, 30 September

This morning beckons warming thoughts of home
with smiles, blue skies and sun now truly ours,
clasped hands still my Love, my gastronome
all-glowing as a field of yellow flowers.
In this fruitful land you were my feast,
my *promenade* 'neath honied cave-dwelt cliff
on ancient water's edge with fair-plumed beast,
my rock enduring as a petroglyph,
ma truffe noir, canard et pâté foie gras,
jugged wine and shaded, tree-lined boulevards
complete, sweet France, with *crème et tarte aux noix*
beneath a pergola of vine and stars.
I kissed your hand, *Chérie*, in Périgord,
mon Petit Chou, the one whom I adore.

Sonnet XVI
King's Court, 4 October

When love cries out a Spring returns to Winter,
shutters closed admit no warmth or praise,
curling leaf returns the Great Provider,
Time does mire these melancholic days.
In this heartscape undeservèd cast,
those blinds reflect, the heated shafts do sear,
yet when a *cri du cœur* makes fit to burst,
in calm each other we must never fear.
My Love relents and with much gentler words
life returns, a softer verdant dawn,
innocence wakes to hear the throng of birds,
hope wells and wills a greater love re-born.
There's only ice or fire when love departs
our kings of kindness and my Queen of Hearts.

Sonnets 16. and 17. *We had*
our only misunderstanding here
and I went away for two days. It
pained us both. The Lady wrote
a poem to me and I was very
touched. I almost didn't open the
envelope because it was enough she
delivered it by hand and had
written my name so beautifully on
it. She sat talking to Sigrid all
afternoon waiting for my return.

Sonnet XVII
Joy Lane, 9 October

Toy Soldier urged Pierrot not pretend.
He'd fallen silent, flute unplayed that week
because he feared he'd lost his Special Friend.
"Chin up!" he cried, "we will your Princess seek."
The pair set off with Dog that eve to rescue
Lublu borrowed by a heartless child.
With Teddies they'd arranged a rendezvous
though they could guard her only when she smiled.
The owls next morn reported Lublu safe,
at the meeting on the old *chaise longue*.
The Dolls then planned a welcome for the waif,
of fireside stories, poetry and song.
That joyous night 'midst twirling in the pen
Pierrot vowed they'd never part again.

27

Sonnet XVIII
John Wilson Park, 16 November

All the Teddies came to Lublu's treat
with love and cuddles for a special dolly.
In celebratory song they growled so sweet,
so pleased to see her well and really jolly.
While Rupert spoke of love and chivalry
that kept the younger dolls and elves enthralled,
Pierrot welcomed friends and made a tea,
as everyone, it seemed, at King's Court called.
That night in dewy cool with moon full grown
a happy Lublu hung her dancing shoes
and hugged a pretty dolly of her own,
a present from her *Beau* on which to muse.
Pierrot played a little lullaby,
the Dollies' smiles told him that he did try!

Sonnet XIX
King's Court, 24 December

So fine a Yuletide Eve of crystalled ice
and gold-rimmed plate and spicy fruit-filled dough,
almond, cinnamon and flush-pink mice,
your warmth and cheer to make the solstice glow.
With childlike glee and pungent warming wine,
my twinkling Star atop a tinselled tree,
without you there is no *auld lang syne*
at this year's end and Christian apogee.
Where berries witness love beyond dispute,
beneath the mistletoe, I wait your kiss
for at this time of mist and mellow fruit
you will for ever be my Season's Wish,
the finest Christmas gift emblazoned gold,
the other Greatest Story ever told!

Sonnet XX
Turin, 14 February (2001)

This day I cannot hide my love's awake
and my *diavolo* does make my plea,
the *signorina's* lips a smile to make
and set impassioned feelings free.
With this disclosure of a ripened heart
and a promised "never-ending kiss,"
I bring a touch of Latin lovers' art
to stir those buds and wake the gentle Miss.
With warming eyes and journey love exhorts,
including posy, card and winning prose,
I convey once more my ardent thoughts
and trust I'll win again my sweetest rose!
Your gracious gift says I'm your Valentine.
To you, therefore, this *bàcio senza fine.*

Sonnet 20. *I have not seen a better presentation of love, affection and romance than the way in which it is done in Italy at* San Valentino.
Returning from a trip to Turin I wanted to bring back cioccolata, fiori, torta *and* pasticcino. *The little red devil did bring a smile to the Lady's lips.*

Sonnet XXI
King's Court, 20 March

If love should fall as rain, then shower-kissed,
we will together find our pot of gold.
By future rose-pink storms we'll not be missed
and never will our fondest thoughts grow cold.
Lovers don't get soaked, only showered,
since this rain does seek, as Cupid's darts,
only those whose love has truly flowered
and rainbows daily touch their caring hearts.
Through saddened eyes and anxious tear drops,
or flashing smile and touch a tremble brings,
'neath cotton clouds where loving never stops,
through sun and storm we'll greet these things.
Blessèd with this wond'rous weather view,
as lightning strikes, love-struck I am with you!

Sonnet XXII
John Wilson Park, 1 April

Oh, how I long to hear my Honey Bee
a-buzzing in my ear, a promised treat,
your fur to trace and stroke and you kiss me
and be smiled upon by nectar sweet.
From silky dawn through lazy afternoons,
I'm driven wild by thoughts of honied sprays
and heady scent of pollen-ripened blooms,
to lick my lips and on your beauty gaze.
Even with the calm of firelight
and gentle slumber after wanderings much,
it starts again, that ageless lovers' rite
as I am deftly woken by your touch.
Yes, Bee Beautiful, my nectar dream,
I Bee King, my Honey, you Bee Queen!

Sonnet XXIII
Leicester, 15 April

On sun-dipped lanes and byways yellow-splashed,
up nodding banks of gold and crocus blue,
in dwellings Spring-flower decked and smile-filled,
my heartfelt Easter thoughts are all for you.
As sunlight dapples, teasing bud and bloom,
its warming rays to prompt again so large
this ritual play of April's vital tune,
your smiles do make their way their loving charge.
And as this vibrant play bursts forth in joy,
we too respond with sun-kissed days so giddy.
You are a Spring itself with which to toy,
an April dazzle, elated, wild, pretty.
The curtain's up on you, my Symphony.
To Spring just in the wings, our sympathy!

Sonnet 23. *I had met Janu and Shanti. Now we were invited to their house for the week. I had to work and so left the Lady in Middle England to meet again the following weekend and bring her home.*
I saw deterioration in her ability to walk but said nothing.

At Easter Time

33

Sonnet 24. *Living together now since I asked over Valentine's supper in a local restaurant if I may, I was beginning to see we should enjoy each other's company while we could.*

This is one of my favourite sonnets. It was a portent.

Sonnet XXIV
King's Court, 15 May

My cherished love, my fragile hour-glass,
too fine to slip before Time's eye unnoticed,
too rare a forfeit of Fate's normal pass
and worthy prize for which to be accounted.
Alas, we know of bodies Time makes light
and we cannot please or plead this master.
Merciless, he'll pace our mortal flight,
not Reaper's ally, just our Maker's marker.
What I must do is nurture every grain,
with passing nod to Vanity and Strife
and ensure through each the full we gain
though with a deeper, gracious bow to Life.
That these sands slip not I will endeavour,
that I may pleasure long your hour-glass figure.

Sonnet XXV
King's Court, 5 July

Shall I compare thee to the rarest rose?
Thou art more precious than this fabled bloom
through which perennial beauty colour flows
from blood-drawn sky to whitest seaborne spume.
Though a joy uplifting weary hearts
our finest flower is wind-blown hue and scent.
You, my Love, are all that love imparts
also here and blessed by God's consent.
Whether water-dropped in shimmered sea
or finest copper-hued in autumn light
the perfect rose no candle holds to thee
whose perpetual grace is pure delight.
Thy beauty fadeth not, my Love's Endeavour.
As flowers are, thou will be held forever.

Sonnet 25. *is one of several under the heading Parodie when grouped. This was the Lady's favourite.*

The question "do you really mean what you've written?" vexed me for a while. One thought that went through my mind almost whimsically was I am not making these up ...

Sonnet 26. *The Lady didn't feel well as we crossed Switzerland in the car and she said she would like to return home as quickly as possible. Only months later did she tell me her health was deteriorating.*

I had planned other excursions on our last few days of holiday and realise my being cross at the time was inexcusable.

Sonnet XXVI
John Wilson Park, 7 August

Once the mighty July flame had spoke,
cutting daily paths through limestone Var,
firing dark damp gorge and stunted oak
tinting lakes a lighter lavender,
you did sparkle, gaiety igniting
all *en route*, north to south on sight,
Provençe, the *Côte D'Azure* not so exciting,
You the glittered holiday delight.
Long-anticipated highs had wooed
but beneath those glaring skies all frazzled,
fire did only quell and cool our mood
though as ever, I in you have revelled.
Home again, you are a gentler Sun.
The call of France this time was not such fun.

Sonnet XXVII
Toddington, 26 August

The sky flares, the Sun does make its bow
and misty curtain cool an English shire.
This matinee did close with sombre vow,
though my love plays on with evening choir.
The day has warmed the chalky downland scarp
and alone at dusk the air's quite rare,
save her laughter as the gentlest harp;
but, deserving of my Loved One's prayer?
As *convulvulus* and ripening berry
jot the hedge and banks of fading field,
I do warm to eyes a-dancing merry
and with thoughts of home and Kentish Weald
I pledge again, if she loves only me,
at every morrow I must worthy be.

Sonnet 27. *is the first with an
extended theatrical metaphor
suggested in Sonnet 23. The Lady
was a pillar of the town's theatre
group and had spent part of her
early years on the stage as actress
and singer.*

*Ironically I saw her becoming
quieter, more introspective but had
no idea what was behind it.*

John Wilson Park,

A tear did slip whe
having tumbled wit
The kindly seamstr
all she needed was

When Pierrot raised
the gathered court
Beneath a watchful
the birds did also s

Sonnet 28. *The Lady tripped in a shop on the High Street that week and hurt her back. The pain got worse and she went to the hospital for tests later that month.*

With her smiling as ever we carried on daily life, planning, giggling sometimes. Friends were still coming regularly to the house but she hardly came shopping or walked the dogs now.

Sonnet XXVIII
John Wilson Park, 15 September

A tear did slip when Lublu hurt her arm
twice now tumbled with the naughty witches.
Kindly Seamstress said "no lasting harm,
all she needs is love and fine new stitches."
Beneath a watchful beaming face, the Moon,
the birds did line and show a friendly wing,
Pierrot raised his flute to rouse a tune,
the gathered courtyard crowd began to sing.
Crickets, bats and owls upon the tiles
even livened up the crispy air
such the chorus brought those lovely smiles
before their Mistress left for her repair.
Pierrot held her tight and kissed her ear.
He was there and nothing need she fear.

Sonnet XXIX
King's Court, 17 November

Night yet before the day to steal away,
breathing silent, bathed in silver raw
from misty courtyard drizzle-cold and fey,
my Sylvan Sprite I gaze upon in awe.
Thus I start this ode as every day,
from moor or wood or shore of foaming gold,
past flowering hedge along Spring's coloured way
where fruits a-ripen as your smiles unfold,
through Summers fresh to dance and Autumn stroll.
Arm-in-arm a foggy eve we slow
and you do warm the hearth of Winter's toll,
setting days of darkened nights aglow;
our timeless journey while you softly sleep,
on which, my Beauty, I do silent weep.

Sonnet 29. The Lady never read this sonnet. It remained in draft and now replaces the original birthday ode I thought weak.

Its sentiment was not a positive one considering her consultant had just referred her to the oncology unit. Reading it at this time would have upset her.

Sonnet XXX
King's Court, 17 December

Star Eternal, lucent night and day
with fine-cut brilliance softened by your heart,
my leading light along the Starry Way,
a youthful shine forever you'll impart;
a witching smile that all does overthrow,
as light cavorting on a flowing stream,
with look and touch to sooth the toughest brow,
that puts the kindness back on which we wean;
the glass through which I see and dream at one
and gem in polished golden glinting crown
to whom I hurry home when work is done
and warmth with which I later rest in down;
who imparts a glowing rosy view,
without whom I'm frost and jade and dew.

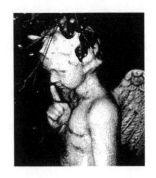

Sonnet XXXI
King's Court, 31 December

What gives rise, my Love, to angels' wings?
Wind-borne flight of moths and butterflies,
tiny restless feather-preening fledglings,
noblesse oblige that Heaven upwards rarefies?
Mystery-moving ways to all but me
and those you love and over whom you watch.
For you wander as God's marvels, free
as angel silence-hushed on finger touch
or cherubs gracing frieze about the rooms
and dancing sunlit-stippled courtyard scene
with all its beauty-blessed all-fragrant blooms
all showing rich deep hues serene.
Just as an angel's wings our spirits lift,
you are also Nature's special gift.

Sonnet XXXII
St. Melluns, 14 February (2002)

As damsels silk-attired and knights lace-ruffed
cast longing eyes like haunted moonlit lawns;
and huddled courtyard doves do wait all-fluffed
while Venus brightens shorter winter dawns,
my Love does also reach to touch my soul,
coaxing smiles, passions kept aglow,
as bud to bloom and horse from shaky foal
through days too short and nights to morn's cockcrow.
All *amoureux* know the month's to flower
and so I pray my Valentine's near won,
with anticipation hour by hour,
trusting not a slip such love's undone.
This day proclaims a year-long vow anew,
from heart and pen of one *inconnu!*

Sonnet 32. *It had been a difficult few months with Margaret suffering from undiagnosed cancer. Prescribed Co-codamol by an overworked doctor she nearly broke down in pain on what should*

have been a romantic weekend in Wales. He prescribed a morphine-based medication on her return which I had to stop her glugging.

A fortnight later, her son rang me at my office and said they had just returned from hospital and I should come home to hear the news.

42

Sonnet XXXIII
King's Court, 31 March

Easter lambs and bunnies come and go,
chocolate eggs and tart with cream much ate
while music, wine and love 'twixt us does flow
reminding me of pleasures since we met.
Then there's laughter, jest and golden smiles,
mischief too with softest eyes and touch,
taking me with joy through all those miles,
such, methinks one never gets too much!
For ever we will laugh, carouse, caress,
enjoy the feast and fare with yellow chicks
while scented buds of pink and white impress
that every gorgeous Spring will be a fix.
On may you reign, my Love whom I had sought,
that we may know and cherish long King's Court!

Sonnet XXXIV
King's Court, 3 April

A precious kiss of gracious Mother Earth,
cherub-lipped and glowing angel-bright
like honied wood with gilded silver laugh.
Iridescent too with feathered might,
now nectar-fed and fuelled and beauty-given,
one God-sped on journey awful stern,
a mighty striving helped by faithful-driven
bearing you aloft with flight so firm,
destined for the place called Chosen Heart,
the mortal shore where kindred souls belong,
where youthful hearts eternal love impart
to hold up life again triumphal strong.
As Spring calls and leaf and bud unsleep,
I am waiting there for you to keep.

Sonnets 33. *and* **34.** *Any Easter fare was probably cancelled, though I can't be sure since the Lady was so hospitable. These sonnets are a clumsy attempt at reassurance, now there was the distinct possibility she was terminally ill. She did not comment on them. It was more a problem with me getting to grips with the situation than her, so far, stoic handling of it.*

Sonnet 35. I drove the Lady to a private clinic in London because she was now also troubled with neuralgia across her face. They were impressed with her pain threshold. I was impressed that Spring  *morning she was ever smiling as we walked a little way along the Embankment under the plane trees. I wrote the sonnet while waiting in the car.*

Sonnet XXXV
London Bridge, 23 April

Golden moments all we spend together,
stored away with thoughts and pleasures seen,
the treasured love of you and I forever
whispered every time we smile and dream.
If sadness ever seemed our joy to crush
it was a sometime gentle measured test
that love does ever rise above and flush
to bond and strengthen friendship at its best.
There's much more that in this chest we'll slip,
some never bettered, though it can't be filled,
and into which in years we'll happy dip
with moments brushed again in which we thrilled.
Let's cherish full these days we spend together,
made first with love to linger on forever.

Sonnet XXXVI
King's Court, 12 May

Lublu lay so wistful sad and still
that Teddy, Horse and Hare did wait awhile
the nursery to stir and cheer to fill,
anticipating soon her precious smile.
Pierrot seemed so distant too this time
but witches' power or not his *Belle* meant all
and like a princess silk and satin fine
she'd rise with full red lips and make the ball
and prove the court her *Beau* she did adore,
that darker corners wouldn't get their chance,
that she would catch all eyes upon the floor
and show she'll always come to play and dance.
Until that evening near did come about,
Pierrot, resolute would pray devout.

Sonnet 36. *The news from the hospital consultant was such I could only embrace the Lady silently when I got home that evening. She had a year to live.*

"It is your job now to keep me cheerful!" she said smiling. Her son said we should consider a round-the-world trip but she had difficulty walking and thought

this would be too much.

She wanted firstly to go to Ireland to visit Tina and Bryan. They loved King's Court, a house the Lady had designed. They built a replica on top of a hill in County Carlow. She also requested a farewell to her beloved Paris and closest friends.

Sonnet XXXVII
King's Court, 18 May

A gentle song does always pass her lips,
my Muse mellifluous in pleasing flow,
a bounty sweet as sighs on pillowslips
love espied with charged ethereal glow.
How graceful too, my Charity, sublime
as supple willow fronds and Pampas plumes
upon this mortal soil, beating time
as wind does airy kiss the whispering blooms.
This land's a lighted stage, my Terpsichore,
an open house and audience encaptured,
a place for flower seasons to explore
with the budding cast also enraptured,
where my shining Love on whom I called,
entranced me so she'll ever be adored.

Sonnet XXXVIII
Northbourne, 15 June

Pierrot held his Lublu's hand inspired,
recalling warm and pungent days abroad,
musing as an English sun had fired
its opening cream and crimson flower chord,
Sweet minuet accented blue and white,
on basket blooms and wafted jasmine scent
to set the courtyard dancing through the night.
Recounting also passioned days they spent
in groves beneath an azure sky a-baking
cypress tree and fruits and flicking tails
among hibiscus, herbs and grapes a-swelling,
reflecting on a joy that never fails,
reminding him his Love, just quiet awhile,
was all these things at home with just one smile.

Sonnet 38. *It was a beautiful June day when I booked a flight to Dublin and Eurostar to Paris. We couldn't venture further. The Lady sat in the courtyard counting her blessings, particularly the home she loved.*

She held my hand and said she didn't want to die, now she had everything to live for.

48

Sonnet 39.

Ireland, fresh and green with 'Celtic Court' looking over the Black Mountains was a tonic. Our long weekend was only marred by an airport baggage hold-up that meant Margaret suffered for some time without medication.

Sonnet XXXIX
King's Court, 1 July

Sweet forgiveness *Éireann* girls so pretty,
my Love's with me, my beauty lacy-fine,
roaming cobbled streets in fair smiled city,
gazing lough and fen stood still in time.
Rare, a countenance that so beguiles
turning heads, hellos and long goodbyes,
with eyes to kindle peaty fireside smiles
and lift those rain-swept fields and aching skies.
Of Celtic stock come home where legends swirl,
she stepped these shores to dwell awhile,
a gem returned to ancient myths impearl,
whose eyes did shine across the Emerald Isle,
a land that poets and romantics miss,
as she who tingles like a stolen kiss.

Sonnet XL
John Wilson Park, 20 July

There were glum faces in the pen today.
Even Golly looked a little pale,
though the Happy Bunnies got their way
in saying their hat was not a shrouded veil.
Lublu wasn't sure if Pierrot cared
and sadly sat with Dog all afternoon.
China Doll enquired how she had fared
the contretemps beneath the kindly Moon.
The Witches cackling, cried he'd never change,
the Dollies chorused he was quite a catch.
When suggestions went through all the range
it was agreed they were a perfect match.
Pierrot took his Lublu's trembling hand,
assuring her their love millennia spanned.

Sonnet 40. *relates to the option Margaret gave me about remaining at King's Court to the end and what I might have to endure. "Don't*

be daft, you're not getting rid of me that easily ..." I replied, to her great relief,

She was pleased that Ingibjorg and her daughter Alexandra-Mist visited from Switzerland in July.

Sonnet 41. *The Lady's spirit lifted during our few days in Paris. I wheeled her around Printemps and the Galeries Lafayette. She looked beautiful in the embroidered skirt she bought, understanding this was the part of her most visible in a wheelchair. A turnaround in her health brought on by her beloved Paris would have been wonderful but it was not to be.*

Sonnet XLI
King's Court, 17 August

Summer's triumph, Autumn's rustic days,
we're not there my Darling, yet a while.
Delight that youth's still here in many ways,
in springing step, full Summer in your smile,
so many season's fruits I've yet to taste
from lips and looks and body sunshine sweet.
Of this bounty nothing I'll let waste,
a meadow flower-edged of ripened wheat.
Plenty more to do and time to spend,
more wind and sun to kiss this wond'rous way,
forever young, tomorrow has no end,
Today's still hand-in-hand with Yesterday.
There will be Winter frosts and snow sublime
that we'll enjoy, as you will still be mine.

Sonnet XLII
K & C Hospital, 12 September

Beneath the slender bowers in sunlit grove,
with fragrant breeze light as lovers' breath
and lately smiling wild end of rose,
we peruse the yellow-russet Autumn heath,
my Love beside me through to Winter now,
my soft catalpa trumpet whispering
and fruit pick-ripe in hedge and tended row
that gives dark mystery to Summer's ring.
Be assured I'm still those boughs bedecked
and branch my tender plant did often hold
in seasons high and low that we have trekked,
through tranquil morning mists and tempests bold
and hearth and table laid for dearest guests
with endless loving warmth with which you're blessed.

Sonnet 42. This relates to the last appointment with her consultant. He spoke to her briefly, fell silent and walked out muttering his registrar would take over. The nervous young woman broke the news there was nothing more the hospital could do. At least they had spared her chemotherapy.

As I lifted Margaret into the car I said this was not what we wanted to hear.

Sonnet 43. *does not hint at the Lady's physical deterioration. After several sonnets that lacked conviction with so much going on at King's Court I concentrated on this one for her birthday.*

She was in good spirits after a week of care in the Hospice.

Sonnet XLIII
King's Court, 17 November

As songs sweet thoughts impart in airy grace
and verse, a harmony of words and soul
that breathes love's images on every place
do cast away the doubt that love is whole;
as Stargazer Lilies, scent sublime
with vibrant hue and majesty combined
that stir the passions and the artist prime
do dispel the myth that love is blind,
these expressions lovers yearning seek
so eloquent uphold my Love Crusade,
for every heartfelt battle, bold or meek
through history for you was surely made.
All love's lexicon and melody
is writ for you, all song and prosody.

Sonnet XLIV
King's Court, 24 November

A lusty chorus all the bears did make.
'Twas time enough to find a Teddy's voice
and show the Dolls they really were awake
in just the way they wanted to rejoice.
As the basses in the nursery throng
with whom their Lublu sang in sweet descant
they practised hard a rousing welcome song,
so pleased they were such some had cause to pant.
Pierrot said he'd fix a competition,
and why not a full-blown *eisteddfod?*
Sense prevailed, the boisterous Teds did listen
and their week-long growling got the nod.
It was "hip, hip" for Lublu home to come
from all who'd missed her love and warmth and fun.

Sonnet 44. *There was one more visit to the hospital for an operation in which a rod was inserted into the Lady's femur. I regarded it as an act of kindness since the surgeon said privately he didn't feel this bone breaking should be added to the trauma of Margaret's last weeks. This he let slip and I was confronted with a harsh reality.*

Sonnet XLV
King's Court, 30 November

A tempest howls, the air does wring its stuff,
a sodden winter-weary set-piece through
with magic mix of wit and word off cuff
and special light from sun and moon to view.
The Summer show's a treat. Baton up,
the daily overture and same enchanting star,
entr'acte to curtain fall, bouquets and sup,
such fans and coterie do journey far.
Dramatis personæ and *diva* one,
her adoring public, gods to stall,
do vocal sit or stand enthralled bar none,
tossing tokens each day's curtain call.
In this, my ever-rapturous review
the accolade's, of course, *Vedette*, for you.

Sonnet XLVI
King's Court, 25 December

At every good, old-fashioned Christmastime
of baubles, coloured foil and pattern clipped
we honour with our cups of love and wine
names immortal, ever-faithful lipped.
But none should lightly treat the Christian cheer
reminding us this birth perpetually
embracing us through every grateful year
is not just feasting, mirth and *bonhomie*,
it is the time of grace for what we share
and thanks our Maker's precious gift of thee
with whom my life's a marvel thoroughfare,
who nurtures love and laughter drawn of me,
such the strength of happiness, I vow,
you will always be beside me now.

Sonnet 46. *The Lady insisted we have a Christmas party. The previous two years had been musical occasions. In years past there had been as many as sixty people at King's Court.*

To my great surprise she appeared at the subdued gathering after a supreme effort of getting up and dressed. She looked like a million dollars and there was spontaneous applause from her friends.

Sonnet 47. *The New Year heralded no joy. I shed a tear reading this poem to the Lady, because she was dying and there was nothing I could do. Braver than I, she remained calm and cheerful despite, as she*  put it, feeling awful. It was for a second time she told me I was a gift from God in the Autumn of her life.

Sonnet XLVII
John Wilson Park, 31 December

Peacefully upon her lace-edged pillow,
twilight grey on cool pink satin sheet,
Lublu's in the land that Time does slow,
savouring his slumbered charges sweet.
Her fine friends did also coo last eve
her rouge-done cheeks and eyes like patterned dishes,
trilling, turning, nodding, truly pleased
that she did cast her basketful of wishes.
So innocent she wakes from Tenderland,
stirred gently now by bars of gold her sleep,
a maiden just let slip her Pierrot's hand,
that he in *crepuscule* did silent weep
awaiting the return his Rag Doll Queen.
He cannot go alone where lovers dream.

Sonnet 48. *I was late with this end-of-year compliment, undecided about what I wanted to say.*

I can't remember much of events at the time, certainly not what I was doing on the motorway and sincerely hope I was not trying to finish it while driving.

Sonnet XLVIII
M25 Motorway, 31 January (2003)

Surely not, my Love, a year all done?
For me, twelve months replete with melting moments
spicy-filled, like deep mince pies and fun
beyond December's Christmas complements.
What next, a Simnel cake and daffodil
all year? Almond scent and colour bright,
that you my days and nights already fill
with year-long taste of Easter's sweet delight?
And what if every day was Valentine's?
Here too I'm blessed! Trinkets to revere
with quiet promises on which love dines,
forget-me-nots such music to my ear.
Fortune shone when you did gracious smile,
though warming through my Maiden took a while!

Sonnet XLIX *(Ragnarök)*
King's Court, 10 February

On empty Asgard's battle-haunted plains,
with solar winds and creeping starlit swell
and pallid Moon and Sun that cools or pains
as cheerless Viking sagas oft do tell;
on lonely Bifrost Bridge in primal mood
I sit in pensive watch a land chilled hollow,
red and raw from Sun just gone to brood,
waiting for those better dreams tomorrow
always brings where love and hope are shared.
My Freya comes to warm this *Fimbulvetr,*
Vanir, Aesir, all around are spared,
Garm falls silent, Fenrir starts to whimper.
Of one goddess *Eddas* never wrote,
my Love, the one that I, by whom, was smote.

Sonnet 49. *is the last poem in which I thought of the Lady as she was early in our relationship. Using Scandinavian apocalyptic mythology was desperation. Once again, care from the Hospice revived her and she was pleased Yelena and her daughter Anastasia came to visit and wheel her around the grounds. They were sadly shocked at her appearance.*

Sonnet 50. *I should have known the Lady would not like this one. My 'backup,' was not much better. Writing poetry was not uppermost in my mind.*

I brought one of the dogs, Bertie, in to the Hospice. He had a tumour. Sadder still was the Lady's comment "the bookies are even odds on which of us goes first ..." Bertie was taken to the vet during the week. Words failed me when the Lady said she wanted to get her death over with as well.

Sonnet L (Valentine 1)
King's Court, 13 February

Come, my Pretty Lass! You're already
all the boys around their Valentine.
I'm the first you kissed and feel heady -
have a chocolate, we've not much time.
Come, my Lovely Maiden, so appealing!
All the world for you is not too much,
let me woo you with romantic feeling -
all I'm asking is a little touch.
Come, my Little Darling, show some willing!
If she knew she wouldn't mind, your mother.
No, I'll never tell a shiny shilling
won your heart and hopefully the other.
Yes, Sweet Ladies, truth a little wavers
in this age-old striving for your favours!

Sonnet LI (Valentine 2)
King's Court, 14 February

Once more red hearts, bouquets and sultry choccies,
window dressing for the tempted male
and those who're bound to spend some pennies
lest their target-arrowed Heart should wail.
And the giggly girls just swapping text
eyeing thoughtful, lacy bras and pants
while others, memory recall long vexed
do yearn to feel their eager youthful wants.
Some regard it as a simple chore,
some consumed in trusting not to fate.
Others destined silent to adore
can only flick through cards and hopeless wait.
I'm so glad my Valentine's at home,
with romance and love that's all our own.

Sonnet 51. *was the last I wrote to the Lady. She had the slip case and 51 cards at her bedside at her death a few weeks later. The saddest moment over those weeks was her distress at dreaming in the Hospice she was to be put away in a toy box in the cellar.*

With concern over my feelings she removed our Irish betrothal ring from her finger and returned it to me. She had smiled and smiled through her illness and was still smiling the last time she closed her eyes.

To M C

Structure of the Sonnet

The sonnet is a form of verse originating in Italy that has settled into one of fourteen lines in iambic pentameter. For those unfamiliar with these technical matters, a pentameter is a line of verse with five feet, or sections. In each section the word, words or syllables have a distinct accent. If the foot is iambic it has an unstressed syllable followed by a stressed syllable. Ă-dóred and dĕ-céive are examples.

If sonnets were written entirely in iambs they would sound monotonous. There is variation of metre, of stresses, within the line. A trochee, for example, is a foot containing one stressed and one unstressed syllable, as mí-ddlĕ and sé-ttlĕ. A spondee is two accented syllables as, Wést-gáte. Westgate Towers would spread over two feet in a sonnet, a spondee followed by a trochee Wést-gáte /Tów-ĕrs /

The first Italian sonnets are referred to as Petrarchan after the work of the poet Francesco Petrarca (1304-1374). They are made up of an octet (eight lines) rhyming *abbaabba,* and sestet (six lines) rhyming *cdecde* or similar. The second part usually answers a problem, or resolves a dilemma presented in the first part of the poem. The Petrarchan sonnet had a major influence on poetry across Europe and was introduced into England in the Sixteenth Century.

The form was adapted and developed for the English language. It evolved into what is now known as the Shakespearean or Elizabethan sonnet. This is made up of three quatrains and a couplet rhyming *abab cdcd efef gg*. A variation in this rhyming scheme comes with the Spenserian sonnet after the work of the poet Edmund Spenser (1552-1599). It follows the English development but brings back the Italian element of linked rhyming thus, *abab bcbc cdcd ee*.

It is slightly less arduous composing verse in the English form but it requires a summary of the spirit of the poem in the last two lines.

Shakespeare's sonnet sequence published in 1609 addressed to a young man and a 'dark lady' is regarded as the finest. Centuries after they were written they are seen less as a sequence of poems about love, more, perhaps about the social period and cultural values.

The originality of Shakespeare's expression and use of language remains unsurpassed. From the Sixteenth Century to the present most other subjects of poetry have been explored in the enduring Elizabethan form.

Ten years on from writing the sequence in this book I have the pleasure yet to come of reading Petrarch's **Il Canzoniere.** These 360 poems, mostly sonnets, he was still re-arranging and improving at his death in 1374. The focus of his passion was the already-married Laura to whom he may never have spoken. I redrafted my sonnets for this book **Poems Writ for Lublu** and plan to write more.

Index of First Lines

Notes

Made in the USA
Charleston, SC
04 September 2015